Our In-Betweens

Athena Snow

BookLeaf Publishing

India | USA | UK

Presentation by *BookLeaf Publishing*

Web: www.bookleafpub.com

E-mail: info@bookleafpub.com

ISBN: 9789395755740

First edition 2023

I dedicate every word to the man I will always love, whatever form it may be.

For all the moments shared, good and bad, I choose to acknowledge everything from the start, and for all those, I am left with a thankful heart.

PREFACE

One winter night, a snow owl was flying through a heavy snowstorm. The poor owl, cold and lost, could not see anything through the blizzard. Suddenly, a branch hit her wing, and she crashed on a pile of snow in the middle of a forest. A few steps away, a traveling reindeer heard the owl's cry and came to the rescue. The reindeer offered company and aided the howling owl. Stuck in cold and lost in the woods, the two shared each other's warmth to survive the cruel night.

After the storm, the owl and the reindeer woke up to branches scattered on the ground and paths erased by the snow. The owl realized that she landed in a foreign place. Having no idea how to start her way, she asked the reindeer if she could tag along just until a way appeared clear for her. Gladly, the reindeer said yes. He told the owl about his plans to reach the highest mountain up north. Since the owl was too broken to fly, the reindeer carried her on his back and continued his journey.

Along the way, the two exchanged their own stories and adventures. The reindeer lent his strength and comfort to the owl, and in return, she guided him through the dark paths. Little did the two know that they had created an invisible bond from every memory they made, and a link was added with every footprint drawn on the ground.

As days passed, the trees grew buds, and the yellows filled the grass. The owl, inspired by the reindeer's determination to reach the peak, started to think of her own map of voyage. With her healing wings, she drew her plans filled with exciting adventures and mischiefs. The owl was happy for a long time, and she forgot about the storm that had broken her wing.

Unexpectedly, a sight stopped the two friends on their tracks. They had entered a wasteland devastated by extreme drought. As they wandered through the chaos, the reindeer stumbled on a big rock on the road. He slipped and crashed on the rough ground. Consequently, the owl fell and landed on her once broken wing, and the nightmare of pain flushed her again. Though pained and scarred, the owl had to help herself up but this time on her own.

Overwhelmed by heat, thirst, and exhaustion, the once lively pair started to see their own needs and sufferings. The reindeer grew tired of walking and wanted to run again, unrestrained and free. On the other hand, the owl missed the feeling of the wind and the view of the limitless horizon. The invisible bond they shared started to fade.

One day, a forked road split their way as though fate wanted to say something. There and then, they both understood that it was time - time to run and to fly again. With heavy hearts, the reindeer and the owl exchanged their goodbyes and went their separate ways.

The reindeer, stronger than before, climbed the highest mountain and leaped on every rock blocking his way, and the owl, bolder than ever, chased the endless horizon of possibilities. Both journeyed carrying the unbreakable chain of their wonderful memories together, and wherever they go, they will always be connected.

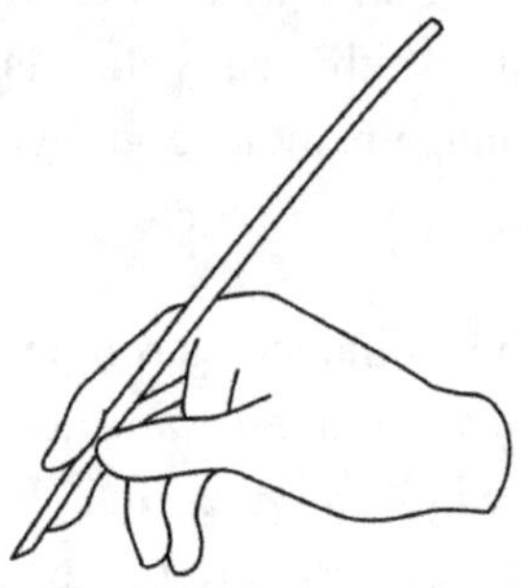

So, It Begins

After a long time, I am writing again
Pouring all emotions: love and pain
All my feelings from beginning to end
And all unspoken and held within.

I am lost in the maze of ambiguities,
A place beyond friendship is uncertainty.
How much power does like need to love?
And what does a special friend need to have?

First Glance

At first, we were just strangers passing by
With short greetings and simple HIs.
Your shell was mysterious that very first time.
Your stares were cold, and you didn't look fine.

Then, I became curious about your glance.
So, I approached you, and I took my chance.
You looked like a book I wanted to read,
Pages filled with wonders and wondrous treats.

Slowly, we got to know each other more
As the days passed by and the owls snored.
You were always so gentle and so warm,
You were simply sweet and filled with charm.

Soon, you started warming up to me too.
You unboxed stories and the things you do.
We stamped precious memories as we go,
And the time was flowing, steady and slow.

The peaceful days we shared by the shore,
The late-night drives 'till morning at four,
The movies and series we checked off our list,
Everything was wonderful, such lovely gifts.

A Chance to Love

Each night I pray to be healed from dismay.
Each night as I lay, I wish the pain away.
I wish I was a little stronger to bear it longer
I wish I could all forget to not end in regret.

I loved you in every way that I could
But you said I feel more than I should.
I loved you in ways you didn't know
But you said I need my feelings to lie low.

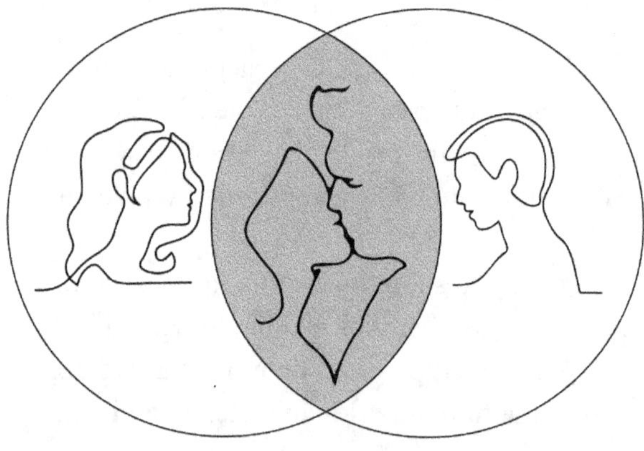

You already shut doors the first time we kissed.
You made it clear "I cannot be more than this".
You said "I'm sorry, more I couldn't do"
But I just wanted a chance to love you.

You said "I only said words you wanted to hear"
That broke me more than the truth I feared.
Your promises then were my reasons to heal
Truth was they were just words for my ears.

You said "I am very lonely and very alone"
So, I stayed and gave your heart a home.
You said "You can hold on to my words with
hope"
So, I held on for as long as I could.

But in the end,
You said that I shouldn't.

Hazelnut Eyes

The man I love is tall and fair, and soft and
comfy like a teddy bear.
And his voice is like the moonlit spring:
deep, calm, and refreshing.
Meeting his eyes is getting lost somehow, to
be lost in the vast hazelnut skies.
Most of the time, he is quiet and tame, and a
mysterious character is his frame.
Yet, deep within is a heart of gold, a nature
of warmth, and stories untold.

Lingering

Late night thoughts
Mind's abuzz and lost
Memories, all in my thoughts
Reasons, all I have lost.

Body is as tired as it can be
Mind is awake but not entirely
I feel so sleepy, yet I could not sleep
My thoughts are raging and running deep.

I think about how you're feeling tonight
Are you asleep or pacing the moonlight?
I think about how I'm feeling tonight
Awake, alone, and out of sight.

It's me, my owl, my bear, and a cup of tea,
And my comfortable Scuderia, warming me.
It's me, my words, and my thoughts that lay,
And my overflowing emotions that always
stayed.

I feel lost, forgotten, and drifting by,
Carrying the pain of the dark night sky.
My heart's crushed, and my tears gone dry.
With all the tears are my silent byes.

I found myself too scared to move
I'm in the middle of this indefinite route.
Neither happy nor in distress,
I'm holding on to my last bit of best.

I am not sure which of the two
Do I miss love, or do I miss you?
Nor sure which one is true
Do I love love, or do I love you?

But if this isn't love at all,
Why does it hurt so much to fall?

What is Love?

Love is the calmness of your voice shouting
my name.
Love is the brightness of your eyes –
deep and tame.
Love is your presence when I'm all alone.
Love is, simply you, my sweet home.

Sad to be Happy

"Hold on to the happy thoughts"
Is your comfort piece.
But did you know that
I've known the good we had
To feel what makes me sad.

The Longest Day

I remember everything about that day
Day filled with laughter, sights, and trains.
A day leaving everything behind,
And travel west to endless fun.

You picked me up at eight-thirty that morning
Like you said the night before.
The ride was an hour forty-five west
Towards the countryside road.

The journey started with a warm tight hug.
Then, off to fill the stead in one big chug.
Poor you, freezing, out in the winter cold,
But you looked dashing, as always, like
sparkling gold.

Our conversation started with updates
that passed,
Regarding school and work and life and lots.
Then, about highways: north, east, west,
and south,
To roller coasters, GO buses, and to how big
are your hands.

My eyes were drowning in all the marvels
around
Of camping cars and buildings, green fields
and barns,
And grey high cliffs, from a distance, that were
actually trees.
First stop: my very first On Route.
(I ran with glee!)

We saw an enormous Canadian moose
wearing a palace guard suit.
So, I took portraits of you like I always do
(you made a dazzling muse).
Surprisingly, you took a picture of me too
That was the first time (it felt so new).

After a lot of driving, we found our sanctuary.
A simple town of fields and greens beyond
ordinary.
Old-school mailboxes lined the empty streets,
And houses owned cars for camping treats.

There was a tiny airport further to the North.
But deeper to its heart was a modern fort.
The center was filled with shops and
medieval-looking lamps.
And the architecture drew scenes of
movie-like banks.

Few more turns and we reached our goal:
A haven of locomotives, trains, and GOs.
There were rows upon rows of stuff to see
From HO layout to cargo car to the simplest tree.

You told me about the different railroad
companies: VIA, CP, CN and more
But Ferromex left the deepest impression
among all.
"Ferromex for Ferrocarril Mexicano"
And you said it with so much gusto.

Luckily, we found a Ferromex autorack
on one of the stands,
You said that you always wanted it, so I
got you one,
A set of tiny engineers and construction
workers too
To remind you of me and the things that I do.

You bought things for your layout to add
Like bridges, graffiti, paints, and wires.
Near the counter were trusses and beams
In tiny cute scales and silver gleams.

There was this cute old couple in the
shop, I found.
They were testing the locomotives: engines
and sounds.
Turned out, locomotives run by the power
from the tracks.
I didn't know they could run backwards
as a matter of fact.

After trains and snacks, we explored the town
more
The Bridges Park had plenty of bridges as
the name holds.
The blanket of snow was hiding the
greens below
And the place was peacefully sleeping in snow.

The drive home felt quick and fast,
Like the map just folded quickly in a flash.
I hoped that time would stop right then,
And I wished for the moment not to end.

But everything becomes meaningful
Because everything ends.

See Me Break

For a long time, I've always known the truth
But I chose to wait for the pain to soothe.
Deep down, I've always known the answer
But I hoped for everything to be better.

I wasn't brave enough to let you go.
I wasn't strong to just go with the flow.
I wasn't bold enough to tell you no.
I wasn't audacious to fool around low.

I showed my pain for you to understand,
And let you be the first to let go and disband
I hoped for you to not give me hope,
And asked: Help me let go of your rope.

You saw me in deep pain
As I cried on you in vain.
You felt me in deep misery
As I held on to you tightly.

You picked me up broken,
But you broke me too in the end.

Québécois

Croissants and coffees and lakeside toasts
Drives and hikes and island tours.

Walks around the tall, orange-bricked walls
That are vibrant like the sunset in summer glow.

Music and trumpet breathe the streets alive
And a couple dancing to the lullabies.

Je me souviens, and I always will
Our vibrant smiles – my happy pill.

Hear My Pleading Heart

For all the times I've been insecure
And asked you questions just to be sure,
And for all the times I've held on too tight
Forgive my ignorance that led us to fights.

For all the times you taught me patience,
And the efforts you give just to be present,
And for all the times you let the wrong go
I appreciate you more than you'll ever know.

For all the times that we said our goodbyes
And again, found in each other's arms,
And for all the times that we tried to heal
I love you then, and I'll love you still.

And if friendship is what we'll ever have,
I'll care for you more, more than I had
But please understand that I need time to heal
To subdue my feelings and the pain that I feel.

If I could turn back time, I want you to know
That I'd still choose you, just you amongst all.
I'd choose to feel everything including the pain
If that'll mean I can love you all over again.

I love you then,
And I'll love you again.

Rawrrrr

Just to let you know
That I love you so.
Just to make you feel
That my love is real.

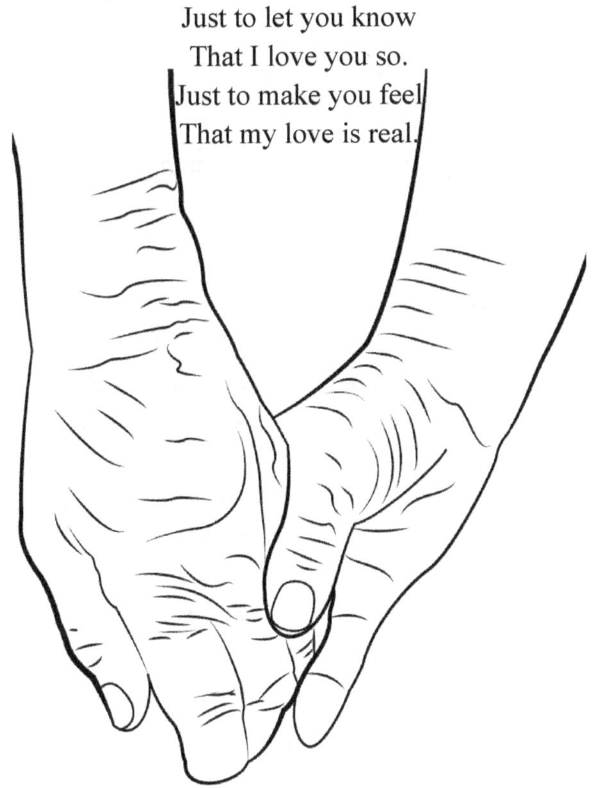

Reasons of Time

I admit, we started on the wrong foot.
The boundaries you drew firmly stood.
Nothing more of whatever we have,
Your priorities first; not ready for love.

I made up reasons for reasons I couldn't find,
And I justified your actions blindly in my mind.
I admit that I should have stood my ground,
A future where love and faithfulness are found.

I forgive you, and I forgive myself too
For everything we chose and choose not to,
For everything we did and didn't do,
And for the love we tried to hold on to.

With You

Every place with you is where I want to be.
You have the power to make me feel safe, bright,
and free.
You always guide me like a lighthouse by the sea.
I am forever grateful, and I wish nothing but to see
you happy.

The Days You Were Gone

Your six short days in another land
Passed by me like counting grains of sand.
Your six wonderful days of sunshine
For me, each second lasted a lifetime.

I was happy to see you free
Going on adventures filled with glee
Off with your friends to different places
Making traces and meeting new faces.

It was peaceful to give myself time
To try new things and have some fun
I met wonderful people in the brief run
People who reminded me of who I am.

Your Truth

I felt it clearly that night
That you love me for what you know is right.
It breaks you more to see me cry,
And it pains you most to hear goodbye.

We were courageous to exchange our truths.
You gave your best for my pain to soothe.
You said not everything in life goes as planned,
But we need to hold on to the good at hand.

You were genuine like you've always been.
Your affection was as honest as I've seen.
Your intentions were sincere as I believed.
And your heart was pure as I perceived.

I saw it clearly that night
That your tears shared my pain inside,
And you wished you could stop all my tears
Like you've been trying to all these years.

If only I could make you feel
How blessed I am to have you here,
How I tried everything to keep you close,
And I regret nothing on this path I chose.

I heard it clearly that night
That our pain whispered the truth we hide.

Sugar Coated Lies

The secrets you hide
Find their way to me somehow
And hurt me with whys.

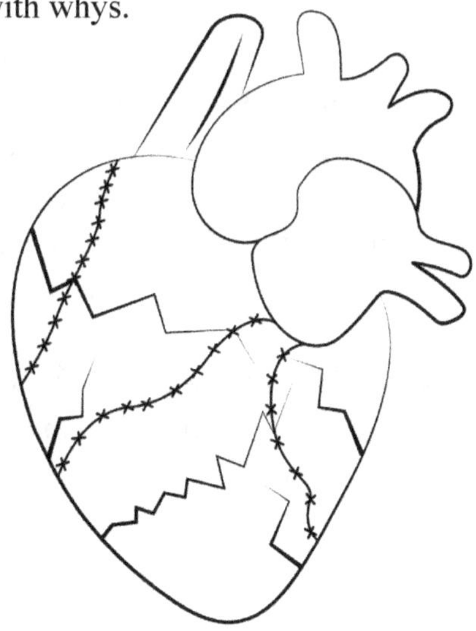

Why are promises used to compensate?
And why isn't everything enough these days?

Bitter Pill

I'll take the heartache for what it truly is
For acceptance is sour and a bitter pill.
"Through it" is the way to survive:
Outgrow the pain, and come out alive.

Love taught me patience to hold on tight
Hold on to what matters most beyond sight.
I learned that love should be selfless for it
to be right
That it matters not the end but to be present
outright.

I learned that life is more than the eyes can see
And love is deeper than the deepest sea.
Time is precious, so set it free
And peace is wonderful as it can be.

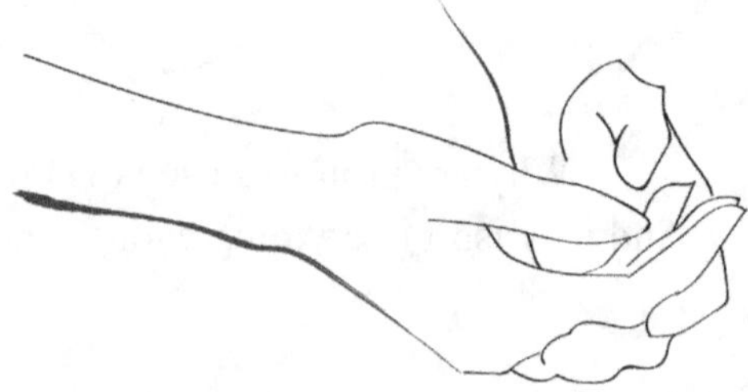

Someday

Thank you for your smiles
And the twinkle in your eyes.
Thank you for the warmth,
And the touch of your hands.

Someday, our paths will re-align.
And again, we'll find them intertwined.
Our promises will soon find their ways
To finally be realized whatever it takes.

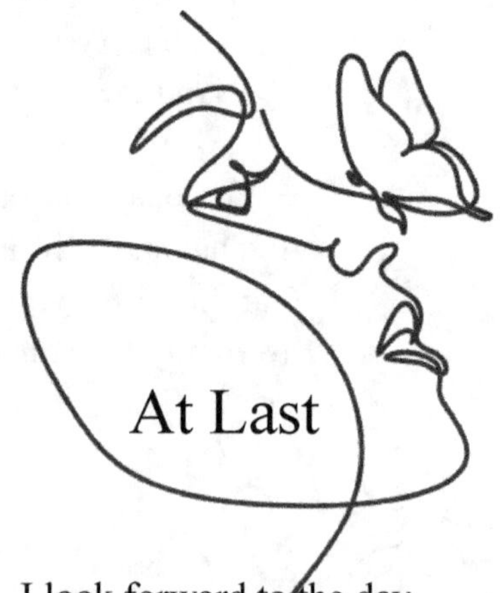

At Last

I look forward to the day
That I can smile in peace and say:
I remember, and I always had.
My heart is healed and no longer sad.

Dear M

Isn't it amazing how the human mind works?
There is more to ourselves that we ought to
know.
We feel different forms of love in this world.
And there are more stories of love untold.

So, come out or just stay in your zone
For nobody knows you as well as your own.
Be effortless and simple, or be extravagant and
grand
Just be the real you, and be your own brand.

Define the life that you want for yourself
But seek out the love from life itself.
Life will be difficult most of the time
But take all the pain and the love that rhymes.

There will always be heartbreaks along the line
But it will yield to understanding that it's okay
to not be fine.
Everything will find its place in this lifetime,
What is meant for us will find its way back – in
time.

But give yourself time to heal
Eat a good meal, or climb up a hill
Healing is hard, and acceptance is key.
Someday, somehow, peace you'll see.

Regret nothing of the love you had.
Remember the joy and pain that passed.
For it is better to have loved, as they always say,
Than not to have loved like a rock at bay.

So, love with everything you have left
But you need to start from within – yourself
For you cannot give what you do not possess.
Be kind, be wonderful, and be always blessed.

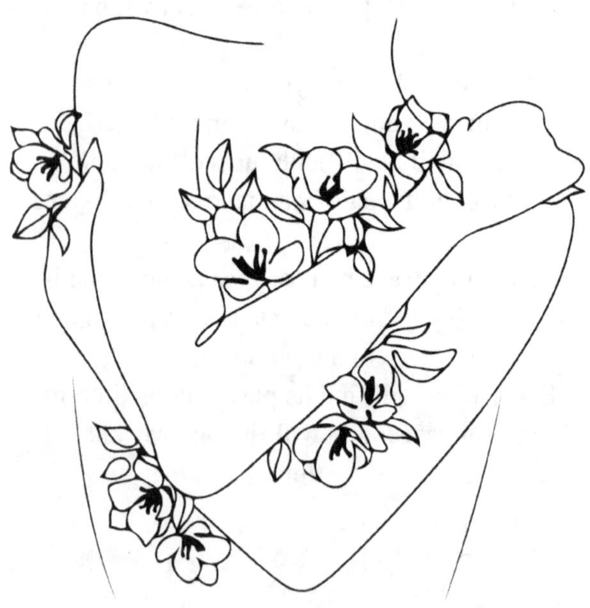

EPILOGUE

The owl once said that it is really heartbreaking that the things that can make her happy are the same things that can make her sad, but she realized that she was looking at the wrong side of the valley all along. Rather, the things that make her sad bring her the purest happiness.

At last, she chose to love the love she had: the joy, the pain, and the in-betweens. And with that, she flew high with her thankful heart, hurt and scarred but not broken.

www.ingramcontent.com/pod-product-compliance
Lightning Source LLC
Chambersburg PA
CBHW061320140726
47998CB00006B/2477